TALL AND SHORT

Tom Hughes

Enslow Publishing
101 W. 23rd Street
Suite 240
New York, NY 10011
USA
enslow.com

Published in 2017 by Enslow Publishing, LLC
101 W 23rd St. Suite 240 New York, NY 10011

Library of Congress Cataloging-in-Publication Data
Names: Hughes, Tom, 1980- author.
Title: Tall and short / Tom Hughes.
Description: New York, NY, USA : Enslow Publishing, LLC, [2017] | Series: All about opposites |
Audience: Ages 5 up. | Audience: Pre-school, excluding K. | Includes bibliographical references and index.
Identifiers: LCCN 2016022721| ISBN 9780766080805 (library bound) | ISBN 9780766080782 (pbk.) |
ISBN 9780766080799 (6-pack)
Subjects: LCSH: Size perception—Juvenile literature. | Size judgment—Juvenile literature.
Classification: LCC BF299.S5 H843 2017 | DDC 153.7/52—dc23
LC record available at https://lccn.loc.gov/2016022721

Printed in China

To Our Readers: We have done our best to make sure all websites in this book were active and appropriate when we went to press. However, the author and the publisher have no control over and assume no liability for the material available on those websites or on any websites they may link to. Any comments or suggestions can be sent by e-mail to customerservice@enslow.com

Photo Credits: Cover, p. 1 (top) costas anton dumitrescu/Shutterstock.com; cover, p 1 (bottom) Irina Barilo/ Shutterstock.com; pp. 3 (left), 12-13 David Allan Brandt/Iconica/Getty Images; pp. 3 (center), 9 Alan Falcony/Shutterstock.com; pp. 3 (right), 10 Top Photo Corporation/Thinkstock; p. 4 James Hager/robertharding/Getty Images; p. 5 claupad/Shutterstock.com; p. 6 Joey Foley/FilmMagic/Getty Images; p. 7 BMacD/Shutterstock.com; p. 8 Rob Crandall/Shutterstock.com; p. 11 Lynn Y/Shutterstock.com; pp. 14-15 Rita Kochmarjova/Shutterstock.com; p. 16 koi88/Shutterstock.com; p. 17 Amy Johansson/Shutterstock.com; p.18 EcoPrint/Shutterstock.com; p. 19 Tam Ryan/Shutterstock.com; p. 20 Peter Weber/Shutterstock.com; p. 21 P.Burghardt/Shutterstock.com; p. 22 Goodshoot/Thinkstock.

Contents

Words to Know

Chihuahua **fire hydrant** **skyscraper**

Short and tall are opposites.

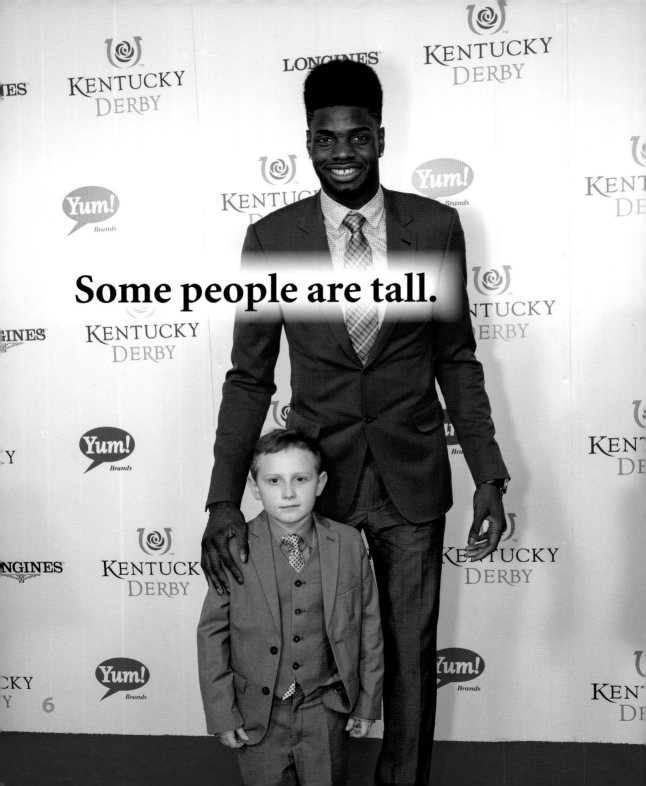

Some people are tall.

Some people are short.

A flagpole is tall.

A fire hydrant is short.

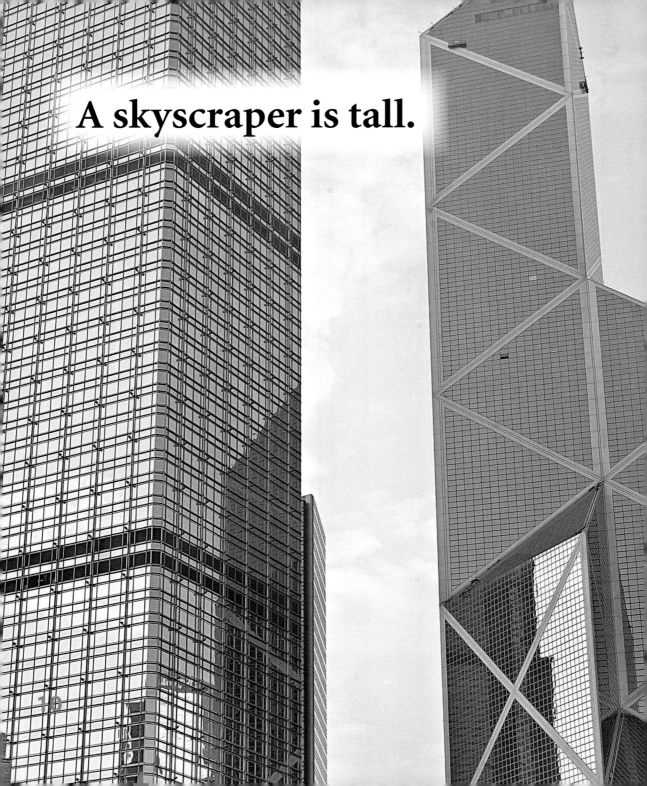

A skyscraper is tall.

A cabin is short.

A Great Dane is tall.

A Chihuahua is short.

A horse is tall.

A pony is short.

Sunflowers are tall.

Pansies are short.

A giraffe is tall.

A chipmunk is short.

Some trees are short.

Some trees are tall.

You will see tall and short every day!

Read More

Katz, David Bar. *Super Heroes Book of Opposites* (DC Super Heroes). New York, NY: Downtown Bookworks, 2013.

Na, Ill Sung. *The Opposite Zoo*. New York, NY: Knopf Books for Young Readers, 2016.

Websites

Enchanted Learning
www.enchantedlearning.com/themes/opposites.shtml
Learn more opposites and do fun activities.

Sesame Street
www.sesamestreet.org/videos?video=6c065d6e-4231-11dd-8df7-9909703b6a2f
Kermit explains tall and short!

Index

Guided Reading Level: B
Guided Reading Leveling System is based on the guidelines recommended by Fountas and Pinnell.

Word Count: 77